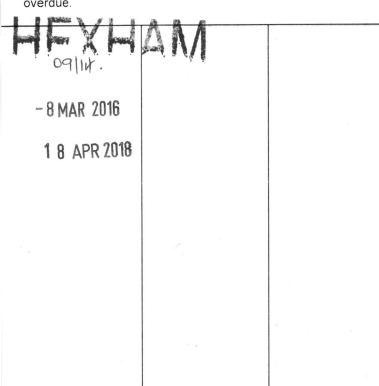

Hello
SEWING!

Simple makes that are just sew

PAVILION

First published in the United Kingdom in 2014 by
Pavilion Books Company Limited
1 Gower Street
London
WC1E 6HD

Copyright © Pavilion Books 2014

ISBN 978-1-91023-104-3

A CIP catalogue record for this book is available
from the British Library.

10 9 8 7 6 5 4 3 2 1

Reproduction by Mission, Hong Kong
Printed and bound by 1010 Printing International Ltd, China

This book can be ordered direct from the publisher at
www.pavilionbooks.com

Contents

Fabrics

The secret of producing a long-lasting and wearable garment is all down to the fabric you make it in. Each fabric gives a garment a different feel and form of drape, and it is vital to know which fabrics are most suitable for the type of garment you plan to make. Choosing fabric can be hard if you do not know what to look for, so spend time browsing in fabric shops and do not be ashamed to ask questions. Take your time to learn and appreciate the qualities of different fabrics. You will quickly become entranced by all the beautiful colours, patterns and textures on display. Fabrics come in different widths: the most commonly available are 112–114cm (44–45in), 140cm (54in) and 150cm (60in).

I love to use fabrics made from natural fibres, such as cotton, linen and silk, and most of the projects in this book are made from these fabrics. There are many places to look for fabrics: dress fabric shops, furnishing fabric shops, remnant specialists, online retailers and market stalls. I'm also very keen on recycling fabric, and for projects that include small pieces of fabric, such as for a pocket or trim, you may be able to reuse old blouses and dresses.

Cotton

A natural fibre. Cotton is a strong, absorbent fibre and cool to wear. Pure cotton is made into a wide variety of fabrics of different weights and finishes; it may also be mixed with other fibres, for example polyester cotton. Cotton voile is a soft, light, gauzy fabric used for blouses and dresses. Cotton lawn is a very fine, smooth, lightweight fabric. Cotton satin has a sheen on the right side.

Silk

A natural fibre. Silk fabrics range from filmy georgette to heavier weights such as silk doupion (also known as dupion). Silk satin is soft with a satiny sheen, and drapes extremely well. Silk crêpe has a surface texture, drapes well and is ideal for dresses and blouses. Silk is an expensive fabric; many types are dry-clean only, but others can be hand-washed in lukewarm water with a special mild detergent. Dry away from sunlight.

Linen

A natural fibre. Linen is very strong and absorbent, and cool to wear; however, it creases easily. It is made in a range of weights from fine, smooth fabrics to heavy, textured weaves.

Wool

A natural fibre. Wool fabrics come in various weights, finishes and textures, from a gauzy voile to suit and coat weights. We generally think of wool as good for providing warmth in winter, but a fine wool fabric is cool to wear in the summer. Washable wools should be cleaned with a special mild detergent, at a low temperature.

Polyester

A man-made fibre. Polyester fabric is very strong and resists creasing, but is liable to pill and can build up static electricity when worn, causing it to cling. Manufacturers can heat-set it into permanent pleats. It is often blended with other fibres such as cotton and wool.

Nylon

A man-made fibre; also known as polyamide. It is lightweight, strong and durable, and does not shrink. It is often blended with other fibres such as wool and viscose. Nylon fabrics are used for clothes, furnishings and other textiles.

Viscose

A man-made fibre created from wood pulp or cotton waste. It is inexpensive and not very strong. It is woven into a variety of fabrics, and may also be blended with cotton, wool or acrylics.

Equipment

You only need a small selection of basic equipment to make the projects in this book. The most expensive item you need to invest in is a sewing machine, but think how much enjoyment you'll get out of it in years to come. Buy the best machine that you can afford, and it is sure to serve you well.

The patterns are printed at a small scale and you will need to enlarge them. To do this, you will need squared paper, a ruler and pencil and scissors for cutting paper. Turn to page 30 for further instructions.

Your sewing box should include a tape measure, dressmaking scissors, safety pins, needles and pins, tailor's chalk or erasable fabric marker and an unpicker (for unpicking stitches).

Haberdashery

Start collecting trimmings – such as braids, ribbons and lace – that inspire you. That way, you can build up a wonderful collection for future projects. Also, keep an eye out for unusual buttons.

Every project requires sewing thread: buy colours to match or contrast with the fabric depending on the effect you are trying to achieve.

Many projects use elastic as a quick and convenient way of gathering fabric into a shape; it is also comfortable to wear. It is available in different widths. Elastic thread is used for shirring (see page 21).

Bias binding is a narrow strip of fabric, cut on the bias. It is used to bind the raw edge of a seam and is available in cotton, polyester or satin, in different widths. Some of the projects use bias binding as a feature, in a contrasting colour to the fabric – such as the edging to a waistline or neckline, or a trim around a pocket. It is also used on interior seams to provide a neat and stable finish that stops the fabric fraying.

Making the projects

At the beginning of each project there is a list of the techniques you will need to use and the pages that describe them. The patterns for the projects appear on the pages after the step-by-step instructions.

Techniques

Seams

French seam

A French seam is one that encloses the raw edges of the fabric within the seam, so there is no need to finish the edges of the seam to stop them fraying.

1 Place the fabric with wrong sides together. Stitch a seam 10mm (⅜in) away from the edge. Trim to 3mm (⅛in) and press the seam open.

2 Fold the fabric back on itself, so the right sides are together and the stitched seamline is on the edge of the fold. Press.

3 Stitch a second seamline, 6mm (¼in) away. Press the seam to one side.

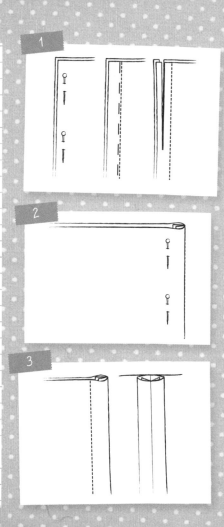

Clipping curves

To reduce bulk and make sure that a curved seam lies flat, little cuts are made in the seam allowance. The seam allowance of a concave curve – for example on a neckline or armhole – is clipped to just above the stitching at regular intervals. For a convex curve, cut tiny, triangular notches out of the seam allowance, to just above the stitching, about 12mm (½in) apart. This will ensure a smooth and flat result when you turn the seam right side out.

The Lace Bow Blouse (above) is constructed with French seams.

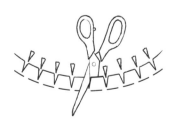

Applying binding

The function of a binding is to enclose a raw edge or seam to prevent the fabric from unravelling. Binding tape comes in various qualities and widths, and is made in materials such as cotton, polyester and satin. All the projects in this book use bias binding, which is cut on the cross and so is slightly stretchy. Choose cotton for a casual look, and satin for a more luxurious finish.

Method 1

1 Open out the binding. Place the right side (outside) of the binding on the wrong side of the fabric, matching edges and folding in the end of the binding if required to neaten it. Pin and tack in position.

2 Machine the two together along the fold line of the binding. Fold the binding up towards the raw edges and press the seam.

3 Fold in the raw edge of the binding along its fold line, then fold the binding over the raw edges of the seam. Pin and tack. Topstitch along the edge of the binding from the right side of the fabric.

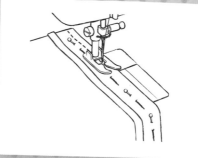

Method 2

1 As for Method 1, but place the right side (outside) of the binding on the right side of the fabric.

2 Fold the raw edge of the binding along its fold line, then fold the binding over the raw edges of the seam. Pin and tack. Hem by hand, catching the binding to the seam allowance so that the stitches do not show on the right side of the binding.

Bias binding is used in the Ruffled Collar (above) to bind the neck edge and form the ties.

Stitches

Slipstitch

This stitch is used to join two folded edges of fabric.

1 Bring the needle out through one folded edge and slip it into the opposite folded edge. Push the needle along for about 6mm (¼in) and bring it out again.

2 Slip the needle back into the opposite folded edge and repeat.

Catchstitch

This stitch looks like a large, loose zigzag and is used to sew two individual sections of a garment to each other.

1 Secure the thread in the first garment section, then make a short horizontal stitch.

2 Bring the needle out and insert into the second garment section. Make another short horizontal stitch, then return to the first garment section and repeat. The thread should not be pulled taut.

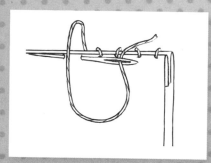

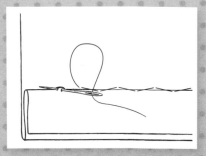

Oversewing

This stitch is also known as overcasting. It is worked over the edge of the fabric diagonally; stitches are spaced evenly and should be the same depth. It is usually used to finish the raw edge of fabric to prevent it from fraying – make stitches fairly deep and work them close together. You can also use it to attach the end of a strap to the inside of a garment facing or casing, making sure that it does not show on the front of the garment. Use doubled thread for extra security.

Topstitch

Topstitching is machine stitching done from the right side of the garment. It may be functional, for example to hold a patch pocket in place, or decorative – or sometimes it fulfils both purposes. Sometimes it is done with a thick thread for a more eye-catching effect.

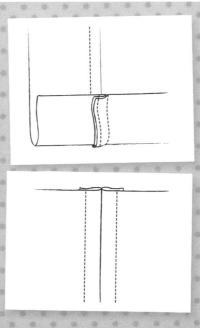

Elastic

Inserting elastic into a casing

This simple casing is made by folding over the edge of the garment.

1 First, turn under the raw edge of the garment by 6mm (¼in) and press. Now fold the edge of the garment to the inside by the required amount. Press. Pin, tack and machine along the folded edge of the casing, leaving a gap of about 5cm (2in) for inserting the elastic.

2 Fix a large safety pin to one end of the elastic, and a smaller one to the other end. Start passing the smaller safety pin through the casing; use the large safety pin to anchor the other end and prevent it from disappearing into the casing.

3 Overlap the ends of the elastic and stitch together by hand or machine. Close the gap in the casing by continuing the machine stitching, matching up with where it left off.

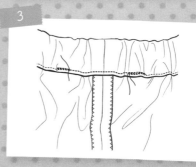

Sewing elastic to fabric

Pin one end of the elastic to the end of the fabric piece to be elasticated, placing the edge 6mm (¼in) away from the edge of the fabric. Stretch the elastic and pin the other end to the opposite end of the fabric piece. Pin the elastic along its length, placing the pins vertically so the machine can sew over them, and stretching it to fit the fabric piece. Use a zigzag stitch to sew the elastic to the fabric. Alternatively, use a long straight stitch.

Shirring

Shirring is a way of gathering fabric, using elastic thread stitched in parallel rows. Stretchy shirring hugs the body and moves with it. It can be used around the bust, waist or hips. The elastic shirring thread goes on the bobbin and normal thread goes in the needle. You may need to tighten the tension on the machine. The space between the rows of stitching affects the finished result: the closer together the rows are, the tighter the shirring.

1 Wind the shirring thread on to the bobbin by hand, stretching it slightly as you do so. Set the stitch length selector to make about eight stitches per 2.5cm (1in). Test the result on a scrap of fabric, and adjust the tension if necessary.

2 Mark parallel rows for the shirring on the right side of the garment. Sew along them, holding the fabric so that it is taut and flat. To secure the ends, stitch backwards for a few stitches over the previous stitches. Alternatively, use a needle to take the top thread through to the back of the fabric, and knot with the shirring thread. When you have finished all the rows, machine across all the knots to secure them.

Construction techniques

Gathering fabric

1 Set the stitch length selector on the machine to the longest stitch length. Machine a row of stitches 12mm (½in) away from the edge, in what will be the seam allowance, leaving a long tail of thread (at least 5cm/2½in) at each end. Alternatively, start the row of stitching by stitching backwards for a few stitches, then stitching forward over them to continue the row; leave a long tail of thread (at least 5cm/2½in) at the other end. Stitch another row 6mm (¼in) from the edge.

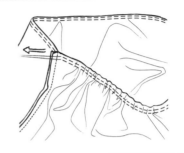

2 Pull the thread tail(s) to gather the fabric to the desired length, making sure that the gathers are distributed evenly. To keep the gathered fabric at the desired length, insert a pin by the thread tail and wind the thread around it, several times, in a figure of eight to secure it.

Making a hem

To make a simple narrow hem on lightweight fabric, press 6mm (¼in) to the inside and machine. Turn over another 6mm (¼in) and topstitch 3mm (⅛in) from the fold.

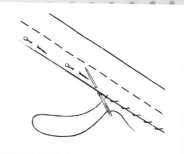

To make a wider hem on medium-weight and heavyweight fabrics, mark the depth of the hem and press to the inside. Turn over 6mm (¼in) to neaten the raw edge, and then press. Finish either by topstitching 3mm (⅛in) from the fold, or work uneven slipstitch by hand – bring the thread out through the fold of the hem, then take a small stitch in the garment, catching just a few threads of garment fabric. Insert the needle back into the hem and push it along the fold a little way. Bring the needle out of the hem and repeat the process.

Making a narrow strap

Knowing how to make a narrow or 'tunnel' strap is very useful. It allows you to create shoulder straps or laces in the same fabric as the rest of a garment or in another fabric that you particularly like. All you need to do is to cut a strip of fabric to the length and width you want, and add a seam allowance of 6mm (¼in) on each edge.

Method 1

1 Fold the strap in half, right sides together. Pin, tack and machine one short edge and along the long edge with a 6mm (¼in) seam. Leave the other short end open. Trim the seams.

2 Fasten a safety pin to the sewn short end, then start pushing the safety pin inwards into the tube of the strap. Feeling the safety pin from the outside, continue to push it through the tube of fabric, smoothing out the fabric as it bunches up, until eventually the safety pin exits the tube at the open short end.

3 Remove the safety pin and press the strap. Turn in the open ends and slipstitch together.

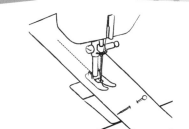

1

Method 2

1 Cut a piece of string the same length as the strap. Fold the strap in half, right sides together, with the string inside. Pin and tack one short end, trapping the string, and continue along the long raw edge of the strap. Leave the other short end open.

2 Machine with a 6mm (¼in) seam, making sure that you do not catch in the string. Trim the seams. Pull the string to turn the strap right side out. Remove string. Turn in the open ends and slipstitch together.

Zips

Zips of different weights and types are used to fasten trousers, pockets, jackets, dresses and skirts; they can also be used as decoration. With a little practice, you'll find that inserting a zip is not as big a challenge as you thought!

Standard zip

You will need to use a zipper foot, which allows you to sew close to the zipper teeth. You can adjust the foot to sew both to the left and the right of the needle.

1 On the seam where the zip will be inserted, place the garment pieces with right sides together. Mark the depth of the zip. The top stop should be 6mm (¼in) below the seamline. Pin, tack and machine a 16mm (⁵/₈in) seam below the zip mark and press open. Press under the same amount on the open edges.

2 Pin the closed zip, right side up, on the wrong side of the garment, with the folded opening edges meeting in the centre of the closed zip. Tack.

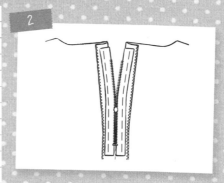

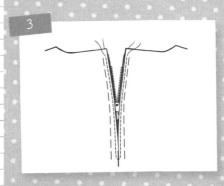

3 Working from the top, machine the garment down one side of the zip, stitching until you have just gone past the end stop of the zip. Stitch across the zip tape and up the other side of the zip to complete.

Concealed zip

A concealed zip is sewn to an open seam – the two garment pieces remain separate – and the seam is stitched when the zip has been inserted. You will need a special concealed zipper foot and a standard zipper foot for the sewing machine. Apply a seam finish if required – such as seam binding – to the raw edges of the garment along the seam where the zip will be inserted.

1 Lay the right-hand garment piece with the right side uppermost. Open the zip. Place the left-hand portion of the zip, face down, on the garment. The top stop should be just below what will be the horizontal waist or neck seamline, and the coil (zip's teeth) should lie along the vertical seamline. Pin and tack. With the concealed zipper foot astride the coil, stitch from the upper edge as far as the slider. Backstitch to secure.

2 Lay the left-hand garment piece with the right side uppermost. Place the right-hand portion of the zip face down as before and pin, tack and stitch.

3 Close the zip. With the two garment pieces with right sides together, pin and tack the seam below the zip. Attach the standard zipper foot. Start stitching just above and to the left of the stitches holding the zip, and complete the seam.

Hook and eye

This two-part fastener consists of a metal hook and loop. One of its uses is to close the tiny gap that remains at a neckline or waistband when you insert a zip. You stitch the hook to one side and the loop to the other.

Making a thread loop

You can make a simple closure for two finished edges by sewing a button on one edge and thread loop on the other. This is the same principle as the hook and eye.

1 Mark the beginning and end of the loop on the garment. Thread a needle and knot the ends of the thread together so you are working with doubled thread. Bring the needle out at the first mark, then insert it at the second, passing under the fabric and bringing it out again at the first mark. Pull gently, so that a loop big enough to fit over the button remains. This is the base loop.

2 Create a loop of thread, passing the needle under the base loop and bringing it out through the loop. Pull to tighten the stitch around the base loop. Continue in the same way along the base loop. When you reach the end, insert the needle at the second mark and finish off the thread on the back of the fabric.

The Princess Collar (above) is fastened with a button and a thread loop.

Working with patterns

The patterns for the garments are in three sizes: small (size 8–10), medium (size 12–14) and large (size 16–18). The small size is printed in black, the medium in red, and the large in blue. The bags and mat are one-size items.

Enlarging the patterns

The patterns have been reduced in scale so that they will fit in the book. Before you can use them, they need to be enlarged to full size. The patterns are printed on a grid to assist with this. The patterns are shown at either a sixth or an eighth of the actual size, and so need to be enlarged by 600 or 800 per cent. You can either do this on a photocopier, or use the grid.

Each square of the grid represents a 6 x 6cm (2½ x 2½in) square at full size. Buy some graph paper or dressmaker's squared pattern paper and establish a grid of 6 x 6cm (2½ x 2½in) squares. Number the squares to correspond to the squares of the pattern. Now draw the shape of each pattern piece, looking at the way the outline of the pattern appears in each square in the book, and reproducing this in the same way on your piece of paper. This enables you to plot the shape of each piece accurately.

Transfer any pattern markings you need, such as labels or notches, to the pattern. Cut out the pieces ready for use.

Fabric grain

Fabric is made up from two sets of yarns, called the warp and weft threads, which are woven together at right angles. This creates a straight lengthways and widthways grain. Along each lengthways edge of the fabric, there is a tightly woven strip called the selvedge.

The way that a pattern piece is placed and cut from a piece of fabric affects the amount of stretch in the piece and the way it will hang when the garment is made up, so it is important to position it correctly. Many of the pattern pieces are marked 'Place on straight grain of fabric'. This grain has very little stretch in it. To prepare the fabric for the pattern pieces, fold it in half lengthways so that the selvedges meet.

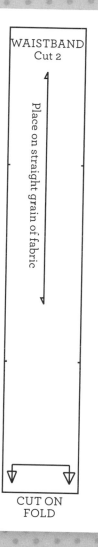

WAISTBAND
Cut 2

Place on straight grain of fabric

CUT ON
FOLD

Laying out the pattern

1 Fold the piece of fabric in half lengthways, so that the selvedges are matching.

2 Pattern pieces should be placed on the straight grain of the fabric (generally lengthways grain). Look for the straight, double-headed arrow that indicates the correct way to orient each pattern piece.

3 Pattern pieces that must be placed on the fold of the fabric are indicated by a double-headed arrow with the arrowheads turned up at right angles. Place the edge of the pattern, where marked, on the fold.

4 Pin the pattern pieces in place. Transfer significant pattern markings to both layers of fabric.

Transferring pattern markings to fabric

You will need to transfer various pattern markings to the fabric, for example to show the position of a pocket. On the pattern these may appear as dots or notches. There are various marking methods.

Tailor's tacks

Special hand stitches made through the pattern and both layers of fabric. You pull the pattern off after you have made the stitch, then cut the stitch so that pieces of thread are left in each layer of fabric.

Tailor's chalk

Use the chalk to draw with; it can be brushed off the fabric when required.

Dressmaker's tracing paper and wheel

Place the paper on the wrong side of the fabric and trace over markings with the tracing wheel.

Erasable fabric marker

Test before use; best used on the wrong side of the fabric.

Patterns

Buttoned flap skirt

When I was designing the projects for this book, I wanted to make a collection of wearable garments that were practical, yet feminine, and this skirt was the first design I drew. From the front it is just a little flared skirt, but the striking buttoned flaps on the back create an element of surprise. The skirt is flattering and easy to wear; the finished length is 52cm (20½in). If you want a longer or shorter skirt, add on to or take away from the straight lower edge of the pattern.

What you need
Fabric – thick cotton, e.g. curtain material: 1m 75cm (2yd) x 112cm (44in)
Matching thread
Bias binding tape: 1m (1¹⁄₈yd) x 25mm (1in) (waist)
Satin bias binding tape: 1m 50cm (1⁵⁄₈yd) x 16mm (⁵⁄₈in) (seam)
Concealed zip: 20cm (8in)
Buttons: 2 x 3cm (1¼in) in diameter
Hook and eye

Sewing machine and foot for concealed zip
Scissors
Needle and pins
Tape measure/ruler
Tailor's chalk/fabric marker

TECHNIQUES

Inserting a concealed zip: see page 27
Making a hem: see page 23
Applying binding: see page 16
Topstitching: see page 19
Slipstitch: see page 18

1 Cut out the fabric according to the pattern on page 41. Apply the satin bias binding to the raw edges of the centre back seam. Insert the concealed zip. With right sides together, stitch the centre back seam. Press the seam open.

2 Sew the two decorative flaps that will be folded to the back of the skirt and held with a button: place the fabric with right sides together, where marked on the side waist, bringing points A and B together. Pin, tack and then stitch along the top of the flap with a 1cm (⅜in) seam. Trim the corner diagonally and clip the seam allowance where A and B meet. Repeat for the other strap.

3 Attach the bias binding for the waist, using Method 1, and for the first stitching along the fold line of the binding, position the fold 4mm (³⁄₁₆in) from the raw edge. Allow the binding to fold up on its folded edge, then fold it over the raw edge of the waist seam to the right side of the skirt. Pin, tack and topstitch. Slipstitch the ends.

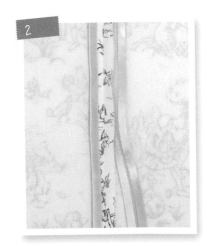

4 Pin the flaps in place on the back of the skirt. Sew a button in the corner of each flap, stitching through the flap and the back of the skirt.

Turn up a hem of 12mm (½in), press, and then turn up the same amount again. Pin, tack and machine. Sew a hook and eye to the waistband binding at the back to complete. This two-part fastener consists of a metal hook and loop. Stitch the hook to one side and the loop to the other.

TIP

You can make an alternative closure for two finished edges by sewing a button on one edge and a thread loop on the other.

Mark the beginning and end of the loop on the garment. Thread a needle and knot the ends of the thread together so you are working with doubled thread. Bring the needle out at the first mark, then insert it at the second, passing under the fabric and bringing it out again at the first mark. Pull gently, so that a loop big enough to fit over the button remains. This is the base loop.

Create a loop of thread, passing the needle under the base loop and bringing it out through the loop. Pull to tighten the stitch around the base loop. Continue in the same way along the base loop. When you reach the end, insert the needle at the second mark and finish off the thread on the back of the fabric.

Buttoned flap skirt: pattern

PATTERN NOTES

Skirt
The front/back of the skirt consists of a single piece of fabric. Place the pattern on the fold of the fabric to cut it out.

Flap
To create the flap, use the dotted lines. With right sides together, fold B to A. Stitch the seam at the top of the flap.

Turn the flap right side out and fold C to D. Secure the flap to the back of skirt with a button.

SEAM ALLOWANCES

The following seam allowances are included:

Back seam: 16mm (⅝in)
Hem: 2.5cm (1in)

Enlarging the pattern
This pattern has been reduced to fit on the page. You will need to enlarge it by 600 per cent before you can use it. This can be done either with a photocopier or by using the grid. See page 30 for more information.

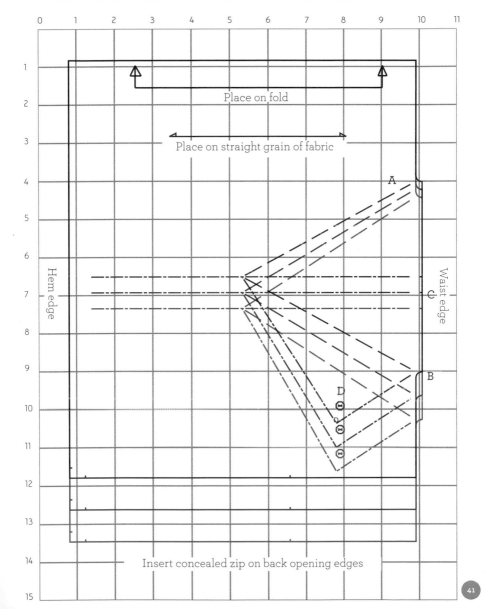

Place on fold

Place on straight grain of fabric

Hem edge

Waist edge

A

C

B

D

Insert concealed zip on back opening edges

41

Snazzy shopping bag

The daily bag dilemma: do I need a big bag or a small bag today? This one is just right – it doesn't look huge, but it's surprisingly capacious; its sturdy plastic handles and heavyweight fabric allow you to cram it full without worrying that the weight will cause the bag to rip. There is a practical pocket on the outside for small things. Look in furnishing fabric shops for fabrics: you're bound to find no end of tempting designs, so why not make a set of bags to accessorize your coats and jackets?

What you need
Fabric – heavyweight cotton or linen:
   50cm (½yd) x 112cm (44in)
Matching thread
Satin bias binding tape: 1m 50cm
   (1⅝yd) x 16mm (⅝in)
Bag handles: 1 pair with approx. 27.5cm
   (10¾in) slit to hold fabric

Sewing machine
Scissors
Needle and pins
Tape measure/ruler
Tailor's chalk/fabric marker

TECHNIQUES

Applying binding: see page 16
Topstitching: see page 19
Slipstitch: see page 18

1 Cut out the fabric (pattern on page 47). Fold the decorative pocket flap with wrong sides together. Pin and tack. Apply bias binding around the curved raw edge; fold in the ends to neaten and then slipstitch. Fold the pocket with wrong sides together. Pin and tack. Apply bias binding to the side raw edges, folding in the ends to neaten. Bind the bottom in the same way. Slipstitch the ends.

2 To attach the flap to the pocket, place the flap with the folded edge towards you and slide the top of the pocket under it. The top of the flap should be 16mm (⅝in) away from the top of the pocket. Pin and tack, then machine close to the edge of the flap. (You could also stitch binding along this join, which will be on the inside of the pocket.) Fold the flap over the pocket and press. Pin in position on the right side of the front of the bag. Tack, then machine close to the edge along the two sides and bottom of the pocket.

3 With right sides together, fold the bag piece and lining piece in half along what will be the bottom of the bag. Pin, tack and stitch the sides of each with 16mm (⅝in) seams. Trim seam. Turn right side out and press.

4 Place the bag inside the lining so the right sides are together and the raw edges at the top are matching. Pin, tack and machine around these opening edges with a 16mm (⅝in) seam, leaving one of the upper edges open.

5 At the V-shape where the two sides meet, stitch again over the first stitching to reinforce it. Clip the seam allowance to the point of the 'V'. Trim

seam. Turn right side out through the opening and press the bag. Turn in the 16mm (⅝in) seam allowance on the open edge, pin and tack.

6 Pass the top of each side of the bag through a handle, turning it over into the inside of the bag. Pin and tack in place. Machine close to the edge.

Snazzy shopping bag: pattern

PATTERN NOTES

Bag
Cut two pieces, one for the bag and one for the lining. Mark position of pocket on the front side of the bag only.

Decorative flap
Fold in half along solid line with wrong sides together, so the broken lines are matching.

Top edges of bag
To attach the bag to the handles, turn each top edge over around a handle and stitch.

SEAM ALLOWANCES
The following seam allowances are included:

Bag and lining: 16mm (⅝in) on all edges.
Pocket and decorative flap: none (edges covered with binding).

Enlarging the pattern
This pattern has been reduced to fit on the page. You will need to enlarge it by 600 per cent before you can use it. This can be done either with a photocopier or by using the grid. See page 30 for more information.

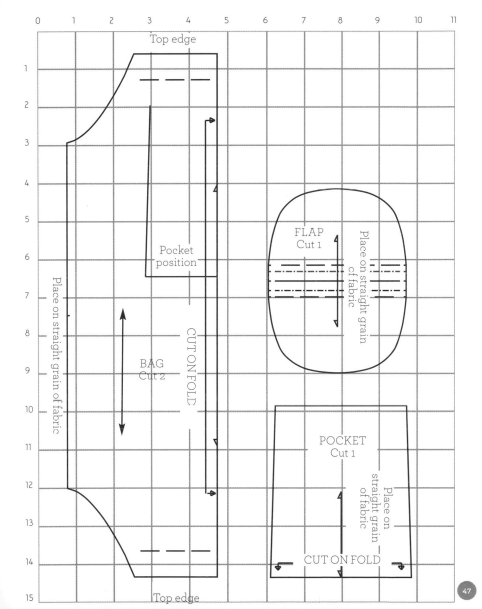

Ruffled collar

This ruffled collar is versatile and great fun to wear: tie it over a plain round or V-necked T-shirt, or use it to add a flourish to a strapless evening dress. It is deceptively simple to make – just three gathered strips of fabric bound at the neckline – but the effect is dramatic. You can make it in about an hour on a Saturday morning, then swan off to impress your friends. Just wait for the compliments.

What you need

Fabric – soft, lightweight cotton,
    e.g. lawn, voile: 1m 50cm (1⅝yd)
    x 112cm (44in)
Matching thread
Bias binding tape: 1m 50cm (1⅝yd)
    x 25mm (1in)

Sewing machine
Scissors
Needle and pins
Tape measure/ruler
Tailor's chalk/fabric marker

TECHNIQUES

Gathering fabric: see page 22
Making a hem: see page 23
Applying binding: see page 16
Topstitching: see page 19
Slipstitch: see page 18

1 Cut three strips of fabric according to the pattern on page 53, for the top collar, middle collar and under collar.

2 Finish three edges of each strip: make a simple narrow hem on the two short edges. Do the same on one long edge.

3 Place the three strips on top of each other, with right sides uppermost and raw edges even. The widest strip, the under collar, is at the bottom; the middle collar lies on top of this; and the narrowest strip, the top collar, is on top. Tack the three pieces together along the raw upper edges. Now gather this neck edge. Pull up the gathering stitches until the neck measures 56cm (22in); secure the gathering threads by winding them around a pin.

4 Cut a single piece of bias binding that will bind the neck edge and form the ties. I have used a piece 1m 25cm (1⅜yd) long, but if you prefer longer ties, increase the length. Apply the binding to the neck edge using Method 1, centring the collar on the binding, but tack instead of topstitching. Pin together the open edges of the binding that form the two ties, turning in the ends. Tack. Now topstitch the entire length of the binding. Slipstitch the ends.

Ruffled collar: pattern

SEAM ALLOWANCES
The following seam allowances are included:

Neck edge: none (edges covered with binding).
Hem on all other edges: 12mm (½in).

Enlarging the pattern
This pattern has been reduced to fit on the page. You will need to enlarge it by 600 per cent before you can use it. This can be done either with a photocopier or by using the grid. See page 30 for more information.

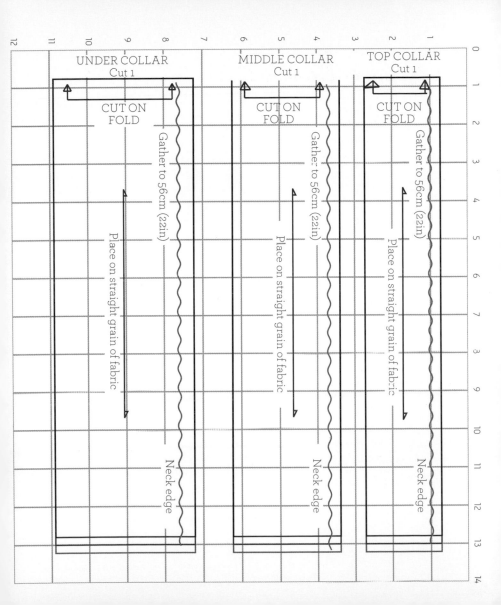

Lace bow blouse

I love designing extremely simple pieces that you can dress up as the mood takes you, and this dainty floral summer blouse was inspired by loose-fitting Japanese garment styles. It is the perfect shape for keeping cool on the warmest of days, and is a cinch to make. It has a boat neckline and a pretty lace tie at the waist – use a single piece of lace or several in different widths. Wear the blouse with a corsage for extra glamour.

What you need

Fabric – lightweight cotton, e.g. lawn, voile: 1m 25cm (1³⁄₈yd) x 112cm (44in)
Matching thread
Lace trim: 2m 25cm (2½yd) x 9-10cm (3½–4in); 6m 50cm (7yd) x 1cm (³⁄₈in) (optional)

Sewing machine
Scissors
Needle and pins
Tape measure/ruler
Tailor's chalk/fabric marker

TECHNIQUES

French seam: see page 14
Making a hem: see page 23
Applying binding: see page 16
Topstitching: see page 19
Clipping curves: see page 15
Slipstitch: see page 18
Oversewing: see page 19

1 Cut out the fabric for the back and front of the blouse according to the pattern on page 59. Join the sides and shoulders with a French seam.

2 Finish the neck and armhole edges with a narrow hem – fold about 6mm (¼in) to the inside, then fold over the same amount again. Pin and tack, then machine in place.

3 Hem the bottom of the blouse by folding 1cm (⅜in) to the inside, then folding over the same amount again. Pin and tack, then machine the hem in place.

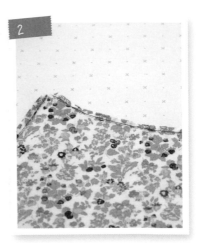

4 Place the centre of the wide piece of lace on the side seam in a suitable position on the outside of the blouse. Pin, tack and machine down the centre of the side seam.

If you wish to add the narrow lace as well, cut it into three equal pieces and arrange the centres over the stitching on the wide lace. Stitch in place. Finish the ends of the lace ties if desired. For cotton lace, just fold over the end and oversew. For synthetic lace, apply binding to the end and then fold over and hem.

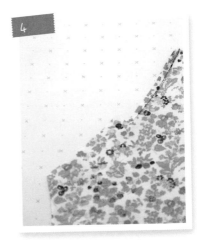

Lace bow blouse: pattern

SEAM ALLOWANCES

The following seam allowances are included:

Shoulder seam: 16mm (⅝in)
Side seam: 16mm (⅝in)
Neck and armhole: 12mm (½in)
Hem: 2cm (¾in)

Enlarging the pattern

This pattern has been reduced to fit on the page. You will need to enlarge it by 600 per cent before you can use it. This can be done either with a photocopier or by using the grid. See page 30 for more information.

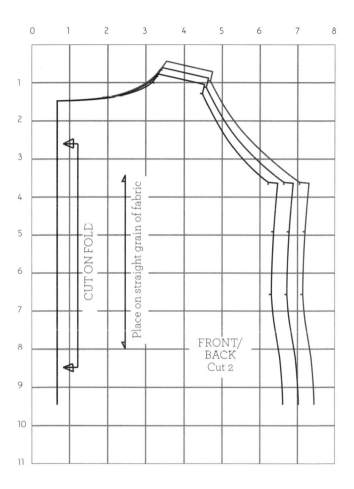

CUT ON FOLD

Place on straight grain of fabric

FRONT/
BACK
Cut 2

0   1   2   3   4   5   6   7   8

Triangle bikini

If you're daydreaming about pale, sandy beaches and crystal blue tropical oceans, picture yourself sashaying along in this itsy-bitsy bikini and pretending not to notice the admiring glances. Get ready for that holiday now – you'll have fun making the bikini and when summer comes you'll be ahead on your holiday wardrobe. I chose a lightweight cotton to enhance the delicate details of the design; the bikini is lined in the same fabric.

What you need

Fabric – lightweight cotton: 1m 75cm
(2yd) x 112cm (44in)
Matching thread
Elastic: 1m (1⅛yd) x 5cm (2in); 2m
(2¼yd) x 5mm (³⁄₁₆in)

Sewing machine
Scissors
Needle and pins
Tape measure/ruler
Tailor's chalk/fabric marker
Safety pins: 2 large, 1 small

TECHNIQUES

Gathering fabric: see page 22
Inserting elastic into a casing:
see page 20
Making a hem: see page 23
Topstitching: see page 19
Making a narrow strap: see
page 24
Sewing elastic directly to fabric:
see page 21

1 Cut out the fabric according to the pattern on page 67. Make the darts in the four bra cup sections. Fold each piece with right sides together, and pin and tack. Stitch the dart, tapering the seam from 1cm (⅜in) at the outer edge to the point of the dart. Press the darts flat.

Now elasticate the underarm and front edges (not the darted edge) of the two lining sections with 5mm (³⁄₁₆in) elastic. Cut four pieces of elastic that are 3.75cm (1½in) shorter than the distance from the lower edge to the apex of the triangle, measured 1cm (⅜in) from the edge of the pattern. Working from the darted edge to the top of the triangle, apply the elastic to the wrong side of the fabric.

2 Make two narrow straps for the neck ties. Lay the two cup fronts with right sides uppermost. Pin the raw end of the strap to the top of the cup and tack in place.

With right sides together, pin the cup front to the cup lining, stretching the elasticated lining to fit the cup front. Tack along the underarm and front edges, being careful not to catch in

the strap. Sew with a 1cm (⅜in) seam. Turn the cup right side out by pulling the strap. Press. Topstitch around the edges using a long stitch.

3 Add the cups to the under-bust bra band. Find the centre of the band. With the cup fronts to the right side of the band, raw edges matching, pin each cup 12mm (½in) away from the centre point. Tack in place; machine with a 1cm (⅜in) seam and press.

Fold the band in half at each end, right sides together. Pin, tack and machine with a 1cm (⅜in) seam, stopping the stitching 1cm (⅜in) from the long raw edge. Trim the seam and turn right side out. Turn in 1cm (⅜in) on both long edges of the band, and bring the folded edges together. Pin and tack. Topstitch the seam.

4 There are two pieces for the pants: use one as the lining. Elasticate the leg edges of the lining as for the bra cup lining in step 1. Cut pieces of elastic that are 3cm (1¼in) shorter than the distance around the leg, measured 1cm (³/₈in) from the edge of the pattern piece.

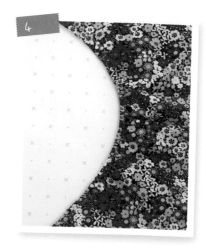

Place the pants and lining with right sides together. Pin, tack and machine the leg edges with a 1cm (³/₈in) seam, as for the bra cup in step 2. Turn right side out and press. Topstitch along the leg edges using a long stitch.

5 Attach the waistband pieces to the pants. Find the centre of each band and of the front and back pants. With the right side of a band to the outside of the pants, pin the pants to the band, matching the centres. Tack and then stitch with a 1cm (³/₈in) seam. Pin the short ends of the front and back band with right sides together. Tack and then stitch with a 1cm (³/₈in) seam; press the seam open. Press under 1cm (³/₈in) on the outer edge of the now circular band, and on the inner edge – continuing from where it is attached to the pants.

6 Fold the waistband over and join the folded edges; pin all around. Tack, then topstitch close to the edge, leaving a gap of about 5cm (2in) above the back pants for inserting the elastic.

Measure out the 5cm (2in) elastic you will need for elasticating the band: hold it around your hips under the hip bone, making sure it is comfortable and not too tight, and add on a little for overlapping the ends. Insert the elastic, then close the casing by completing the topstitching on the band.

Triangle bikini: pattern

PATTERN NOTES

This pattern fits an A cup. To increase the cup size to a B cup, draw a parallel line around each side 6mm (¼in) from the original pattern. Add a further 6mm (¼in) increase per cup size for a C cup and D cup.

Bra cups

Cut four pieces, two for the bra and two for the lining.

Pants

Cut two pieces, one for the pants and one for the lining.

SEAM ALLOWANCES

The following seam allowances are included:

Bra cups, all edges: 1cm (⅜in)
Bra straps, all edges: 6mm (¼in)
Bra band, all edges: 1cm (⅜in)
Pants, all edges: 1cm (⅜in)
Waistband, all edges: 1cm (⅜in)

Enlarging the pattern

This pattern has been reduced to fit on the page. You will need to enlarge it by 800 per cent before you can use it. This can be done either with a photocopier or by using the grid. See page 30 for more information.

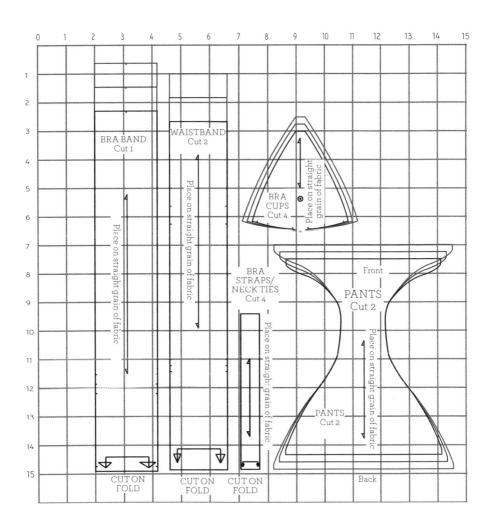

Cute culottes

This skirt-cum-shorts makes a great summer staple – loose and comfortable to wear, and ideal for picnics, cycle rides or lounging around the garden. The unusual shape gives you the fullness of a skirt, but you don't have to worry about the hem blowing up on a windy day because it's a pair of culottes! It features a sweet ruched patch pocket on the front. Choose a soft, lightweight fabric so it will drape flatteringly on the body, as there is no shaping around the hips. Team the culottes with a plain vest, a pair of flip-flops and a roomy bag and head out to make the most of a summer weekend.

What you need
Fabric – soft, lightweight cotton:
    1m 50cm (1⅝yd) x 112cm (44in)
    (culottes)
25cm (¼yd) x 112cm (44in) (pocket)
Matching thread
Elastic: 1m (1⅛yd) x 25mm (1in); 25cm
    (¼yd) x 10mm (³⁄₈in)

Sewing machine
Scissors
Needle and pins
Tape measure/ruler
Tailor's chalk/fabric marker
Safety pins: 1 large, 1 medium

TECHNIQUES

French seam: see page 14
Inserting elastic into a casing: see page 20
Making a hem: see page 23
Clipping curves: see page 15
Topstitching: see page 19

1 Cut out the fabric according to the pattern on page 73. Stitch the side seams with a French seam. Make the waistband casing by folding over 4cm (1½in) and pressing under 6mm (¼in) on the raw edge. Measure out the 25mm (1in) elastic you will need for elasticating the waist: hold it around your waist, making sure it is comfortable and not too tight, and add on a little for overlapping the ends. Insert the elastic, then close the casing.

2 Stitch the gusset with a French seam. Hem the legs: turn 6mm (¼in) to the inside and machine. Turn over another 6mm (¼in) to conceal the raw edge and machine again.

3 Place the two pocket pieces with right sides together. Pin, tack and machine the top of the pocket with a 1cm (³⁄₈in) seam. Press the seam open. Cut a 13cm (5¹⁄₈in) piece of the 10mm (³⁄₈in) elastic and pin to one end of the wrong side of the pocket, just next to the seam. Gently stretch the elastic to fit all the way across, pinning at intervals. Tack, then machine, stretching the elastic as you sew.

4 Fold the pocket along the top seam, with right sides together. Pin and tack around the sides and bottom. Machine all the way round with a 1cm (³⁄₈in) seam, leaving a 5cm (2in) gap for turning. Clip the curves. Turn the pocket right side out and press. Slipstitch the gap to close it. Pin and tack in place on the culottes (I have set it at a slight angle). Topstitch around the sides and bottom 3mm (¹⁄₈in) from the edge.

Cute culottes: pattern

PATTERN NOTES

Pocket

There is one pocket. Cut two pieces, one for the pocket and one for the lining. Mark the position of the pocket on the front of the culottes, on the left side only.

Waistband

On the waistband edge, fold over 4cm (1½in) and on the raw edge of this, press under 6mm (¼in). This forms a casing for the elastic.

Gusset

There is a notch on the pattern to mark where the gusset finishes and the leg opening begins.

SEAM ALLOWANCES

The following seam allowances are included:

Side seam: 16mm (⅝in).
Waistband casing/hem: 4cm (1½in)
Hem/gusset: 12mm (½in).
Pocket, all edges: 1cm (³/₈in).

Enlarging the pattern

This pattern has been reduced to fit on the page. You will need to enlarge it by 600 per cent before you can use it. This can be done either with a photocopier or by using the grid. See page 30 for more information.

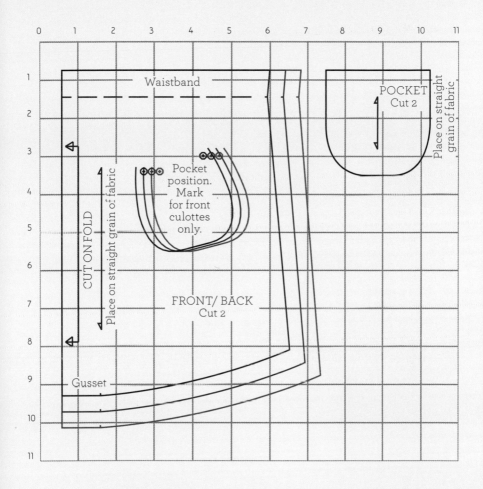

Waistband

POCKET
Cut 2

Place on straight grain of fabric

CUT ON FOLD

Place on straight grain of fabric

Pocket position. Mark for front culottes only.

FRONT/ BACK
Cut 2

Gusset

Princess collar

This chic, elegant collar will make you feel like a princess. It will make an excellent pick-me-up for a plain black dress or top: you can instantly transform a utilitarian look into something altogether more individual and dressy. Slip it into your bag, together with a pair of heels, on days when you're going straight out after work – an instant and chirpy solution to wardrobe angst!

What you need
Fabric – linen or cotton: 1m 75cm (2yd)
    x 112cm (44in)
Matching thread
Bias binding tape: 1m (1⅛yd)
    x 2cm (¾in)
Button: 1cm (³/₈in) in diameter

Sewing machine
Scissors
Needle and pins
Tape measure/ruler
Tailor's chalk/fabric marker

TECHNIQUES

Gathering fabric: see page 22
Applying binding: see page 16
Clipping curves: see page 15
Slipstitch: see page 18
Making a thread loop: see page 28

1 Cut out the fabric according to the pattern pieces on page 79. Make the upper ruffle: fold in half, wrong sides together, and press. Gather the upper raw edge. Pull up the gathers to fit the lower edge of the upper collar. With raw edges together and right sides facing each other, pin the ruffle to the lower edge of the upper collar. Tack, then machine with a 1cm (⅜in) seam. Clip the curves.

2 Make the lower ruffle in the same way. Sew it to the lower edge of the lower collar. Clip the curves after machining.

3 With the wrong side uppermost, pin the lower edge of the upper collar to the right side of the top of the lower collar. Tack. Machine with a 1cm (⅜in) seam.

Now add the facing. Turn the collar to the wrong side. Pin the right side of the lower edge of the facing to the gathered edge of the lower ruffle; tack. With the lower collar piece uppermost, machine along the seamline again, stitching through all the layers. Clip the curves. Turn the facing to the right side and press.

4 Tack the upper edge of the facing to the upper edge of the upper collar. Apply the bias binding tape to this neck edge using Method 1. Slipstitch the ends of the binding.

To fasten the collar, sew a button on one side and work a thread loop on the other.

Princess collar: pattern

SEAM ALLOWANCES
The following seam allowances are included:

Collar facing, all edges: 1cm (⅜in)
Upper collar, all edges: 1cm (⅜in)
Lower collar, all edges: 1cm (⅜in)

Enlarging the pattern
This pattern has been reduced to fit on the page. You will need to enlarge it by 800 per cent before you can use it. This can be done either with a photocopier or by using the grid. See page 30 for more information.

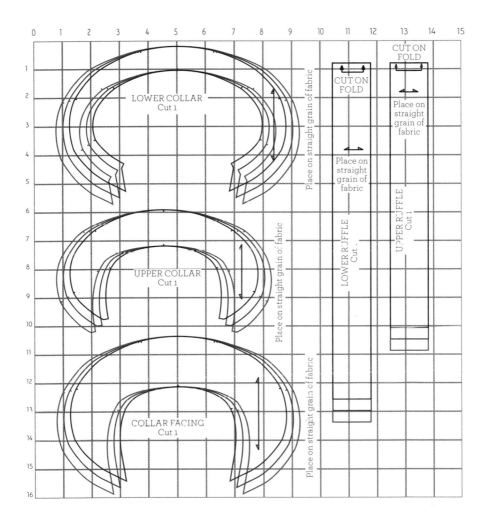

LOWER COLLAR
Cut 1

UPPER COLLAR
Cut 1

COLLAR FACING
Cut 1

Place on straight grain of fabric

Place on straight grain of fabric

Place on straight grain of fabric

CUT ON FOLD

CUT ON FOLD

LOWER RUFFLE
Cut 1

Place on straight grain of fabric

UPPER RUFFLE
Cut 1

Place on straight grain of fabric

Summer dress

A summer dress in a classic vest shape – simple, striking and easy to wear. For me, the design brings back happy childhood memories of long, sunny days and the vibrant summer dresses that I wore. It is a very easy dress to make, because the neck and armholes are finished with bias binding tape. A tie belt adds definition to the waistline; it also features a contrasting fabric on the ends for a stylish twist. The skirt is knee-length; if you want a longer or shorter skirt, add on to or take away from the hem edge of the pattern. The design works well in a bold pattern, as the front and back sections are each a single piece, so you can make the most of all those jazzy prints that are out there.

What you need
Fabric – cotton (dress and main part
   of belt):
Small: 2m 25cm (2½yd) x 112cm (44in)
Medium: 2m 25cm (2½yd)
   x 112cm (44in)
Large: 2m 75cm (3yd) x 112cm (44in)
Fabric scraps – cotton (belt ends)
Matching thread
Satin bias binding tape: 3m (3¼yd)
   x 2cm (¾in)

Sewing machine
Scissors
Needle and pins
Tape measure/ruler
Tailor's chalk/fabric marker

TECHNIQUES

French seam: see page 14
Making a hem: see page 23
Applying binding: see page 16
Topstitching: see page 19
Slipstitch: see page 18

1 Cut out the fabric according to the pattern pieces on page 85. Join the sides and shoulders of the dress with French seams.

Make a hem by pressing 1cm (³⁄₈in) to the inside at the bottom of the dress, then turn over the same amount again. Pin, tack and topstitch.

2 Apply bias binding to the neck and armhole edges, using Method 2. Make a tuck in the binding as you feed it around the V-shape of the neckline. When you turn the binding over the raw edge, hold it in place, then turn over the edge again so the binding is on the inside of the garment and doesn't show on the right side of the dress. Pin and tack. Topstitch the binding close to the edge.

3 Fold a belt end in half with right sides together. Pin, tack and machine one side edge with a 1cm (³⁄₈in) seam. Press the seam open with your fingers and pin the right side of the top of the belt end to the right side of the belt. Tack and stitch with a 1cm (³⁄₈in) seam. Repeat at the other end of the belt.

4 Fold the main part of the belt in half with right sides together. Pin and tack from one end of the belt to the other. Machine with a 1cm (³⁄₈in) seam, leaving a gap of 8cm (3in) for turning. Turn right side out. Slipstitch the gap to close it.

Summer dress: pattern

SEAM ALLOWANCES
The following seam allowances are included:

Side seam: 16mm (⁵/₈in)
Shoulder seam: 16mm (⁵/₈in)
Neckline: 1cm (³/₈in)
Armhole: 1cm (³/₈in)
Hem: 2cm (¾in)
Belt pieces, all edges: 1cm (³/₈in)

Enlarging the pattern
This pattern has been reduced to fit on the page. You will need to enlarge it by 800 per cent before you can use it. This can be done either with a photocopier or by using the grid. See page 30 for more information.

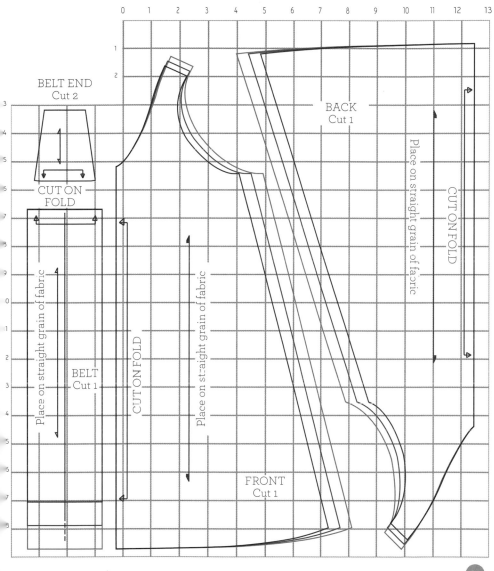

BELT END
Cut 2

CUT ON FOLD

BACK
Cut 1

Place on straight grain of fabric

CUT ON FOLD

Place on straight grain of fabric

BELT
Cut 1

CUT ON FOLD

Place on straight grain of fabric

FRONT
Cut 1

Strapless bikini

This delightful bikini provides a little more coverage than the one on page 60. Cotton bikinis are comfortable to wear and dry quickly. I have chosen a soft, fine cotton in a charming tiny geometric floral print; the end result is a bikini with a cute retro feel. The elasticated bra top expands to a perfect fit, and the soft frill at the top is a flattering feature. The bikini is lined throughout in the same fabric. If you really fall in love with the bikini fabric, why not buy an extra length to use as a sarong? Just hem it around the edges.

What you need
Fabric – soft, lightweight cotton:
Small: 1m 50cm (1⅝yd) x 112cm (44in)
Medium: 2m (2¼yd) x 112cm (44in)
Large: 2m (2¼yd) x 112cm (44in)
Matching thread
Bias binding tape: 2m (2¼yd) x 2cm (¾in)
Elastic: 2m (2¼yd) x 6mm (¼in)

Sewing machine
Scissors
Needle and pins
Tape measure/ruler
Tailor's chalk/fabric marker

TECHNIQUES

Inserting elastic into a casing: see page 20
Making a hem: see page 23
Applying binding: see page 16
Topstitching: see page 19

1 Cut out the fabric according to the pattern pieces on page 91. Take the fabric for the bra top and fold it in half widthways, with right sides together. Pin, tack and stitch the short ends with a 1cm (³⁄₈in) seam. Press the seam open. Fold the circle of fabric in half, with wrong sides together, matching the raw edges, and press.

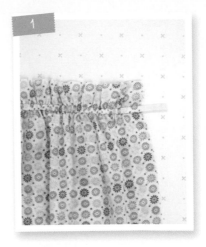

Now make the casing for the upper piece of elastic. Machine a line of stitches 3cm (1¼in) away from the top (folded) edge of the bra top, leaving a gap for inserting the elastic. Stitch another row parallel to this, 1cm (³⁄₈in) below it, leaving a gap in the same place.

Measure out the elastic you will need: hold it around your chest under your arms, making sure it is comfortable and not too tight, and add on a little for overlapping the ends. Insert the elastic, then close the casing.

2 Tack the raw edges at the bottom of the bra top together. Make a hem by pressing 1cm (³⁄₈in) to the inside of the bra top, then folding over the same amount again. Tack, then machine close to the edge, leaving a gap for inserting the elastic. Measure and insert the elastic as before, then close the casing.

3 Make the pants and the lining. For each one, place the front and back pants with right sides together, then pin, tack and stitch the sides and gusset with 1cm (³⁄₈in) seams.

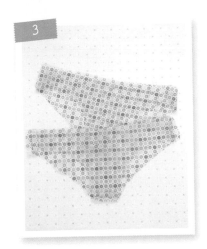

Press the seams open. Turn the lining inside out, then place inside the pants. Pin and tack the pieces together around the top and leg edges.

4 Apply bias binding to the top and leg edges, using Method 2. When you turn the binding over the raw edge, hold it in place, then turn over the edge again so the binding is on the inside of the garment and doesn't show on the right side of the bikini. Pin and tack. Topstitch the binding close to the edge.

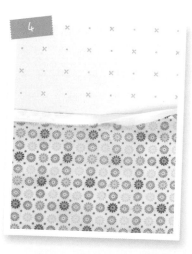

Strapless bikini: pattern

SEAM ALLOWANCES
The following seam allowances are included:

Bra top, short edges: 1cm (³/₈in)
Bra top, long edges: 2cm (¾in)
Pants, gusset and sides: 1cm (³/₈in)
Pants, waist and legs: 1cm (³/₈in)

Enlarging the pattern
This pattern has been reduced to fit on the page. You will need to enlarge it by 800 per cent before you can use it. This can be done either with a photocopier or by using the grid. See page 30 for more information.

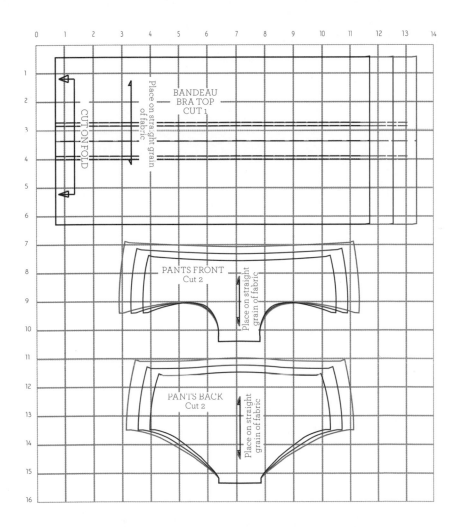

BANDEAU
BRA TOP
CUT 1

CUT ON FOLD

Place on straight grain
of fabric

PANTS FRONT
Cut 2

Place on straight
grain of fabric

PANTS BACK
Cut 2

Place on straight
grain of fabric

Slinky strapless dress

Women who appreciate good, simple cuts and fabulous fabrics that show off their curves will love this gorgeous strapless number. I have used a stunning brown and orange floral silk satin, which flows over the body and drapes beautifully. The hemline is elasticated to give a slightly puffed effect. It has an asymmetric buttoned belt in a geometric design, which provides a funky contrast to the floral print of the dress. This dress is very versatile: wear it with sandals on a summery day, or dress it up with jewellery and heels for evening or special-occasion wear.

What you need

Fabric – soft and silky, e.g. silk satin (dress):
Small: 1m 50cm (1⅝yd) x 112cm (44in)
Medium: 1m 75cm (2yd) x 112cm (44in)
Large: 1m 75cm (2yd) x 112cm (44in)
Fabric – medium-weight silky, e.g. synthetics (belt):
Small: 1m 25cm (1⅜yd) x 112cm (44in)
Medium: 1m 25cm (1⅜yd) x 112cm (44in)
Large: 1m 50cm (1⅝yd) x 112cm (44in)
Matching thread
Elastic: 1m 25cm (1⅜yd) x 50mm (2in); 1m 25cm (1⅜yd) x 6mm (¼in)
Interfacing: 1m 50cm (1⅝yd) x 90cm (35½in) medium weight, iron-on
Button: 3cm (1¼in) in diameter

Sewing machine
Scissors
Needle and pins
Tape measure/ruler
Tailor's chalk/fabric marker
Safety pins: 1 large, 1 medium and 1 small

TECHNIQUES

French seam: see page 14
Inserting elastic into a casing: see page 20
Making a hem: see page 23
Topstitching: see page 19
Making a narrow strap: see page 24
Slipstitch: see page 18

1 Turn to page 97 for the pattern for the dress. When laying out the fabric to cut it, fold it across its width (112cm/44in). Cut out the piece for the dress and fold in the same way; join the raw edges with a French seam.

Make the hems for the top and bottom of the dress, which also form casings for the elastic. For the top, press 7cm (2⅞in) to the inside and turn under 1cm (⅜in) on the raw edge. For the bottom, press 2.25cm (⅞in) to the inside and then turn under 1cm (⅜in) on the raw edge. Pin, tack and machine along the folded edge of each casing, leaving a gap of about 5–8cm (2–3in) for inserting the elastic.

2 Measure out the elastic you will need for the top of the dress: hold it around your chest under your arms, making sure it is comfortable and not too tight, and add on a little for overlapping the ends. Insert the elastic, then close the casing. Do the same for the bottom of the dress: overlap the ends of the elastic until you get the effect you

want – the shorter the elastic, the greater the puffiness at the base of the dress. Remember that you also need to be able to walk!

3 Make the belt loop: cut a piece of fabric 10 x 3cm (4 x 1¼in). Fold in half lengthways, with right sides together. Pin, tack and machine the long edge with a 6mm (¼in) seam. Turn right side out (both short ends are left open).

Cut a piece of interfacing the same size as the belt and iron it to the wrong side of the belt. On the right side of the belt, position the loop between the notches, with raw edges even. Stitch in place with a 6mm (¼in) seam.

4 Fold the belt with right sides together, and pin and tack around the raw edges. Machine with a 1cm (³⁄₈in) seam, leaving a gap of about 8cm (3in) for turning. Turn right side out and slipstitch the gap to close it. Try on the dress, put the belt around your waist and mark the position needed for the button. Sew on the button.

Slinky strapless dress: pattern

SEAM ALLOWANCES

The following seam allowances are included:

Side seam: 16mm (⅝in)
Hem/casing, bust edge: 7cm (2⅞in)
Hem, bottom edge: 2.25cm (⅞in)
Belt, all edges: 1cm (⅜in)

Enlarging the pattern

This pattern has been reduced to fit on the page. You will need to enlarge it by 800 per cent before you can use it. This can be done either with a photocopier or by using the grid. See page 30 for more information.

BELT
Cut 1

Top of dress

DRESS
Cut 1

Place on straight grain of fabric

CUT ON FOLD

CUT ON FOLD

Place on straight grain of fabric

Hem of dress

97

Shoulder bag

This bag almost qualifies as a rucksack, because you can cram so much in it; however, the long shoulder strap is worn across the body and over one shoulder, distributing the weight and leaving you with your hands free. There is a handy outer pocket for items that you need instant access to. The bag and strap sections are cut in a single piece for ease of construction. Make this bag now – it's so useful that you'll wonder how you ever managed without it!

What you need

Fabric – thick cotton or linen:
   2m 50cm (2⅝yd) x 112cm (44in)
Matching thread
Bias binding tape:
   3m 50cm (3¾yd) x 16mm (⅝in)

Sewing machine
Scissors
Needle and pins
Tape measure/ruler
Tailor's chalk/fabric marker

TECHNIQUES

Applying binding: see page 16
Topstitching: see page 19

1 Cut out the fabric according to the pattern pieces on page 103. Pin the pocket with wrong sides together. Tack and then stitch around the curved edge with a 1cm (³/₈in) seam. Turn right side out and press. Apply bias binding to the raw edge of the top of the pocket, using Method 1 and folding in the ends to neaten.

2 Place the pocket on the front bag piece and pin in position. Tack, then topstitch close to the edge around three sides, leaving the top open.

3 Join one pair of front and back bag pieces to make the outside of the bag, and the other pair to make the lining. To do this, place with right sides together, then pin, tack and sew with a 1cm (³/₈in) seam. Sew right around the outer edge of the bag and strap, leaving the hole in the centre open. Do the same with the lining. Press. Turn the bag right side out; leave the lining wrong side out.

4 Slip the lining inside the bag, so the wrong side of the lining faces the wrong side of the bag, the seams of the outer edge of bag/strap and lining/strap match, and the raw edges are even. Pin and tack together along the raw edges of the strap and the straight edge of the top of the bag. Apply bias binding around the raw edges of the straps and opening edges of the bag, using Method 1, and making a tuck in the binding as you feed it around corners.

Shoulder bag: pattern

SEAM ALLOWANCES
The following seam allowances are included:

Bag: 1cm ($^3/_8$in)
Pocket: 1cm ($^3/_8$in)

Enlarging the pattern
This pattern has been reduced to fit on the page. You will need to enlarge it by 800 per cent before you can use it. This can be done either with a photocopier or by using the grid. See page 30 for more information.

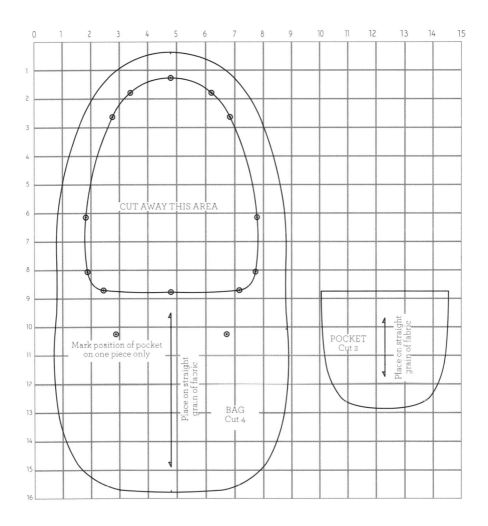

CUT AWAY THIS AREA

Mark position of pocket
on one piece only

Place on straight
grain of fabric

BAG
Cut 4

POCKET
Cut 2

Place on straight
grain of fabric

Rosette belt

This belt is a great way of using scraps of fabric that you love but that are too small for other projects. The instructions are for making a belt 5cm (2in) wide and 1m 80cm (2yd) long, which is long enough to tie with a bow at the back. If you would prefer a wider (as pictured here) or longer belt, which you could wrap around the body several times, adjust the fabric quantity and dimensions accordingly. The width of the two belt fabric pieces needs to be twice the desired finished width of the belt. Add 1cm ($^3/_8$in) seam allowance on all edges.

What you need
Fabric – cotton (belt, 5cm/2in wide):
Small: 1m (1$^1/_8$yd) x 112cm (44in)
Medium: 1m 25cm (1$^3/_8$yd)
    x 112cm (44in)
Large: 1m 25cm (1$^3/_8$yd) x 112cm (44in)
Fabric scraps (rosette)
Matching thread

Sewing machine
Scissors
Needle and pins
Tape measure/ruler
Tailor's chalk/fabric marker
Compass

TECHNIQUES

Gathering fabric: see page 22
Applying binding: see page 16
Clipping curves: see page 15
Slipstitch: see page 18
Making a thread loop: see page 28

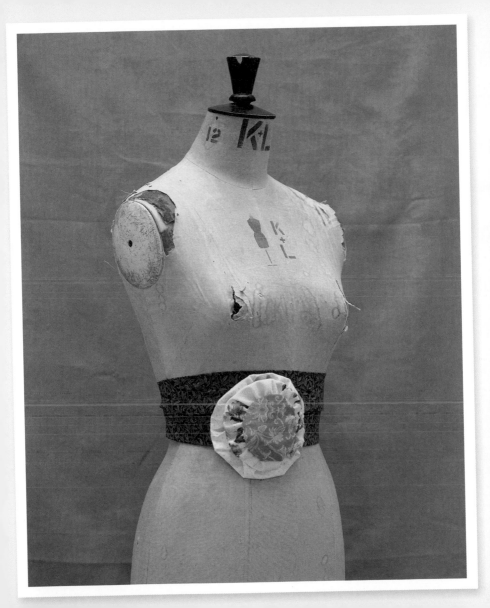

1 Cut out the components according to the pattern on page 109. The rosette is made up of three circles of fabric. Run a gathering thread around the edge of each, place it over the appropriate cardboard shaper, and then pull up the thread to make a puffy, rounded shape. Press gently with your fingers.

2 Assemble the rosette. Place the largest shape with the gathered side uppermost. Pin the medium shape on top of it, the same way up. Use catchstitch to sew the underside of the medium shape to the top of the large shape. Work the stitches 16mm (⅝in) away from the edge of the medium shape, so they don't show, all the way around. Place the small shape on top, gathered side underneath. Fix to the medium shape in the same way as before.

3 To make the belt, join the two pieces by placing two short ends with right sides together, and stitch with a 1cm (³⁄₈in) seam. Press the seam open. Fold the belt with right sides together; pin, tack and sew around the raw edges with a 1cm (³⁄₈in) seam, leaving a gap for turning. Turn right side out and press. Slipstitch the gap to close.

4 Sew the rosette to the belt by hand, catching it securely to the belt in several places by sewing through the bottom of the rosette (so it doesn't show on the front) and into the belt. Use a double thickness of thread for added strength.

Rosette belt: pattern

PATTERN NOTES
Shapers
There is a shaper for each rosette. Cut these out in cardboard and use them to help form the shape of the rosette.

SEAM ALLOWANCES
The following seam allowances are included:

Belt, all edges: 1cm ($^3/_8$in)

Enlarging the pattern
This pattern has been reduced to fit on the page. You will need to enlarge it by 600 per cent before you can use it. This can be done either with a photocopier or by using the grid. See page 30 for more information.

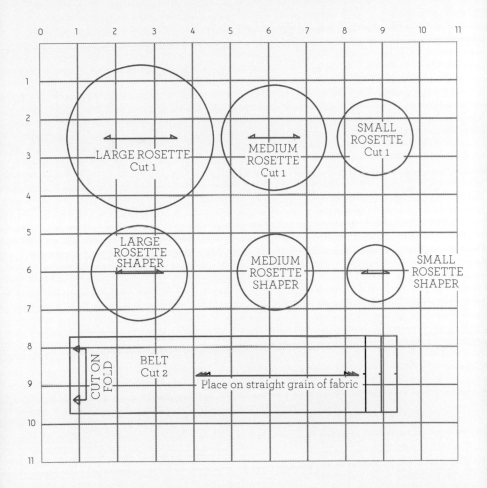

LARGE ROSETTE
Cut 1

MEDIUM
ROSETTE
Cut 1

SMALL
ROSETTE
Cut 1

LARGE
ROSETTE
SHAPER

MEDIUM
ROSETTE
SHAPER

SMALL
ROSETTE
SHAPER

CUT ON FOLD

BELT
Cut 2

Place on straight grain of fabric

Camisole top

This easy, wearable camisole top is a classic. The shirred midriff gently gives it shape, while providing a comfortable fit; the double shoulder straps in contrasting fabric are a distinctive twist. Made up in a pretty sprigged print to echo a garden of summer flowers, you'll look cute and remain cool on sultry days. Wear with beaten-up jeans for casual glamour, or team with a flowing skirt for a more elegant look.

What you need

Fabric – soft, lightweight cotton (camisole):
Small: 75cm (⁷⁄₈yd) x 112cm (44in)
Medium: 1m 25cm (1³⁄₈yd) x 112cm (44in)
Large: 1m 25cm (1³⁄₈yd) x 112cm (44in)
Fabric: 25cm (¼yd) x 112cm (44in) cotton (straps)
Matching thread
Shirring elastic: 1 reel
Elastic: 1m (1yd) x 25mm (1in)

Sewing machine
Scissors
Needle and pins
Tape measure/ruler
Tailor's chalk/fabric marker
Safety pins: 1 large, 1 medium and 1 small
Piece of string (optional)

TECHNIQUES

French seam: see page 14
Inserting elastic into a casing: see page 20
Making a hem: see page 23
Topstitching: see page 19
Clipping curves: see page 15
Slipstitch: see page 18
Shirring: see page 21
Making a narrow strap: see page 24
Oversewing: see page 19

1 Cut out the components according to the pattern on page 115. Stitch the side seams with a French seam. Make a hem around the bottom of the camisole by folding 12mm (½in) to the inside; press. Fold over the same amount again, pin, tack and machine.

2 Sew four parallel rows of shirring stitches, 6mm (¼in) apart, all the way around the camisole, below your bust and above your waist. The pattern gives guidelines for the position of the shirring; however, you may prefer the shirring a little higher up the camisole if you have a small bust cup size, and lower if you have a large cup size, in order to accommodate the bust better.

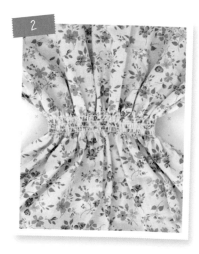

3 Make the casing for the top of the camisole by folding over 4cm (1½in) and pressing under 6mm (¼in) on the raw edge. Measure out the elastic you will need for the casing: hold it around your chest under your arms, making sure it is comfortable and not too tight, and add on a little for overlapping the ends. Insert the elastic, then close the casing.

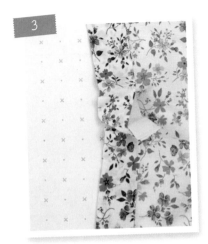

4 Follow the instructions for making a narrow strap, and make four straps. Attach the straps to the back of the camisole – a pair for each shoulder. Oversew securely to the casing by hand. Try on the camisole, bringing the straps over your shoulders. Pin in place on the inside of the front of the camisole. Take the camisole off and stitch the front ends of the straps to the camisole in the same way as for the back.

Camisole top: pattern

PATTERN NOTES
Bust edge casing
On the bust edge, fold over 4cm (1½in) and on the raw edge of this, press under 6mm (¼in). This forms a casing for the elastic.

SEAM ALLOWANCES
The following seam allowances are included:

Side seam: 16mm (⅝in)
Hem/casing, bust edge: 4cm (1½in)
Hem, lower edge: 2.5cm (1in)
Straps, all edges: 6mm (¼in)

Enlarging the pattern
This pattern has been reduced to fit on the page. You will need to enlarge it by 600 per cent before you can use it. This can be done either with a photocopier or by using the grid. See page 30 for more information.

STRAPS Cut 4

Place on straight grain of fabric

CUT ON FOLD

Place on straight grain of fabric

Fold up for hem

FRONT/ BACK
Cut 2

Fold in for bust elastic casing

Attach straps here

Silky skirt

This luxurious skirt is a good project to start with if you're new to sewing. There is no zip to insert – the waistband ties at the side, giving a stylish finish – and the ends of the ties cover the slit opening that allows you to pull on the skirt. The gathers add structure to the silky fabric and produce the lovely puffed shape of the design. Match with chunky knits and thick tights during the winter months, or a sheer blouse and hosiery for evening glamour. The finished length of the skirt (excluding the waistband) is about 50cm (20in): if you want to make it longer or shorter, add to or take away from the lower edge of the pattern.

What you need

Fabric – soft and silky, e.g. silk satin, synthetics: 2m (2¼yd) x 112cm (44in)
Matching thread
Bias binding tape: 50cm (20in) x 18mm (¾in)
Elastic: 1m (1⅛yd) x 2cm (¾in) wide

Sewing machine
Scissors
Needle and pins
Tape measure/ruler
Tailor's chalk/fabric marker
Safety pins: 1 large, 1 medium

TECHNIQUES

French seam: see page 14
Gathering: see page 22
Inserting elastic into a casing: see page 20
Making a hem: see page 23
Applying binding: see page 16
Topstitching: see page 19

1 Cut out the fabric according to the pattern on page 121. Run gathering stitches along the waist edge of the skirt. Pull up the stitches until the material is your exact waist measurement plus 1cm (⅜in) ease; wind the thread around a pin to secure. Measure 15cm (6in) down from the waist on each side seam and mark. Stitch the side seam, as far as the marks, with a French seam. The open part will form a slit at the top of the skirt.

2 Finish the slit by binding each edge. Cut two pieces of bias binding tape, each 16cm (6¼in) long. Apply the binding to each side of the slit, folding in 1cm (⅜in) of binding at the lower end of the slit to neaten it. Press each bound edge to the inside of the skirt.

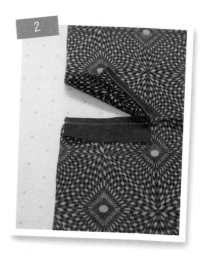

3 Make the waistband by folding it in half with right sides together. Press. Press under 1cm (⅜in) on each long edge.

4 Pin the skirt to the waistband with right sides and raw edges together, placing the skirt centrally on the waistband so that the two tie ends are equal. Stitch the gathered edge with a 1cm (⅜in) seam.

Fold the waistband in half with right sides together. Pin, tack and stitch along each short end and around to where it meets the skirt, with a 1cm (⅜in) seam. Trim the seam allowance, and trim the corners diagonally. Clip the seam allowance where the stitching ends. Turn the waistband the right way out and press. On the inside of the skirt, turn under 1cm (⅜in) on the waistband and catch to the seam allowance by hand. Press. Topstitch the lower edge of the waistband if you wish.

5 Make the hem, which also forms a casing for the elastic: fold 4cm (1½in) to the inside of the skirt and press. Press under 1cm (⅜in) on the raw edge. Follow the instructions for making a casing and inserting elastic, lapping the ends of the elastic until you have the effect you want.

Silky skirt: pattern

PATTERN NOTES

Hem
On the hem edge fold over 4cm (1½in), and on the raw edge of this press under 1cm (³/₈in). This forms a casing for the elastic.

SEAM ALLOWANCES
The following seam allowances are included:

Side seam: 16mm (⁵/₈in)
Waist seam: 1cm (³/₈in)
Hem/casing: 4cm (1½in)
Waistband, all edges: 1cm (³/₈in)

Enlarging the pattern
This pattern has been reduced to fit on the page. You will need to enlarge it by 800 per cent before you can use it. This can be done either with a photocopier or by using the grid. See page 30 for more information.

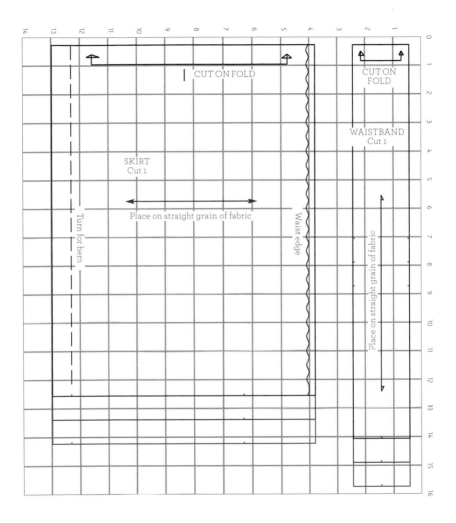

CUT ON FOLD

SKIRT
Cut 1

Place on straight grain of fabric

Turn for hem

Waist edge

CUT ON
FOLD

WAISTBAND
Cut 1

Place on straight grain of fabric

Celebration table mat

If I weren't a fashion designer, I would be a chef, because I love cooking and entertaining. You may think that you have no use for table mats until you have a dinner party and realize that they would be just the thing to add a striking style note to the dining table. This mat is colourful, different, and good to look at while you eat. It is intended to provide a decorative focus on the table – use it under a floral centrepiece or a beautiful display of fruit; it does not provide a heat-absorbing surface
for hot dishes.

What you need
Fabric – thick cotton: 75cm (⅞yd)
    x 112cm (44in)
Matching thread
Fusible interfacing – medium weight:
    75cm (⅞yd)
Satin ribbon: 9m 25cm (10⅛yd) x 5cm
    (2in) in each of two colours
Satin bias binding tape: 1m 50cm
    (1⅝yd) x 2cm (¾in)

Sewing machine
Scissors
Needle and pins
Tape measure/ruler
Tailor's chalk/fabric marker

TECHNIQUES

French seam: see page 14
Inserting elastic into a casing: see page 20
Making a hem: see page 23
Topstitching: see page 19
Making a narrow strap: see page 24
Slipstitch: see page 18

1 Cut out the components according to the pattern on page 127. Fuse the interfacing to the wrong side of one of the circles of fabric, following the manufacturer's instructions.

Place the two circles of fabric with right sides together, and pin and tack around the circumference. Stitch with a 1cm (⅜in) seam, leaving a gap for turning. Cut angled slits in the seam allowance to help the seam lie flat, then turn the mat right side out. Turn in the seam allowance on the gap and slipstitch to close. Topstitch around the mat.

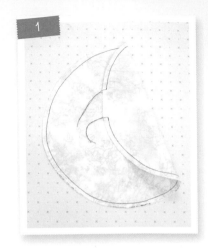

2 Place the outer shaper in the centre of the mat. Cut eleven green and eleven white outer strips of ribbon, fold in half and lay around the outer edge of the mat, with the folded edge at the edge of the mat. Work all the way around the shaper, alternating colours and overlapping the ribbons slightly. Pin the ribbons together, but not to the mat. Tack close to the raw edge of the ribbons.

3 Remove the ribbons from the mat and apply bias binding to the raw edges using Method 1. Turn in the raw ends to neaten them where the binding meets, and overlap slightly. Pin and tack the ribbon circle to the mat. Topstitch along the top edge of the binding.

4 Cut six green and six white inner ribbons for the inner circle, and make in the same way, using the inner shaper and binding with bias binding. Place in the centre of the mat and topstitch along the top edge of the binding.

Celebration table mat: pattern

PATTERN NOTES

Mat

Cut two in fabric, for the mat and its backing. Use the pattern to cut one piece of interfacing also.

Shapers

Cut out an inner and outer shaper in cardboard. Use them to help with the placement of the ribbons.

SEAM ALLOWANCES

The following seam allowances are included:

Mat: 1cm (⅜in)
Ribbons: 1cm (⅜in)

Enlarging the pattern

This pattern has been reduced to fit on the page. You will need to enlarge it by 600 per cent before you can use it. This can be done either with a photocopier or by using the grid. See page 30 for more information.